ENGLISH CONSORT

TREBLE VIOL, SOPRANO OR TENOR REC
FLUTE, OBOE OR VIOLIN

T0085261

PLAYBACK+

Speed • Pitch • Balance • Loop

To access audio visit:
www.halleonard.com/mylibrary

Enter Code
3880-3771-6656-7073

ISBN 978-1-59615-335-6

Music Minus One

EXCLUSIVELY DISTRIBUTED BY

HAL•LEONARD®

Visit Hal Leonard Online at
www.halleonard.com

Contact us:
Hal Leonard
7777 West Bluemound Road
Milwaukee, WI 53213
Email: info@halleonard.com

In Europe, contact:
Hal Leonard Europe Limited
42 Wigmore Street
Marylebone, London, W1U 2RN
Email: info@halleonardeurope.com

In Australia, contact:
Hal Leonard Australia Pty. Ltd.
4 Lentara Court
Cheltenham, Victoria, 3192 Australia
Email: info@halleonard.com.au

CONTENTS

English Consort Music

As heard on the audio, embellishments are often added not only to the top voice,
but inner voices as well as harpsichord, in accepted renaissance practice.

FANTASIA

Giovanni Coperario

MMO 3359

The flute may be used throughout this record, except for the B below Middle C
which occurs in the second section of "Semper Dowland Semper Dolens".

SEMPER DOWLAND SEMPER DOLENS

John Dowland

* Occasional discrepancies between lute and viol parts suggest that the lute was not used when all five viols were present.

*A in the original.

THE KING OF DENMARK'S GALIARD

John Dowland

THE EARL OF ESSEX GALIARD

John Dowland

*The note values of this bar are doubled in the original,
making two bars for the Lute to the Viol's one.

MMO 3359

M. HENRY NOEL HIS GALIARD

♩ = 120   6 taps (2 neas,) precede music.

John Dowland

M. GILES HOBIES GALIARD

John Dowland

M. NICHOLAS GRYFFITH HIS GALIARD

John Dowland

= 116   6 taps (2 meas.) precede music.

M. THOMAS COLLIER HIS GALIARD

With 2 Trebles

John Dowland

CAPTAIN DIGORIE PIPER HIS GALIARD

* The repeat marks - a small 2 above each double bar - appear only in the lute part.
** F in the original: probably a misprint.

MMO 3359

M. BUCTON'S GALIARD

John Dowland

♩ = 126   6 taps (2 meas.) precede music.

MRS. NICHOLS ALMAND

John Dowland

* **The lute part contains four redundant quavers at this point.**

M. GEORGE WHITEHEAD HIS ALMAND

𝅗𝅥 = 84   4 taps (2 meas.) precede music.

John Downland

CANZON

William Brade

♩ = 76   4 taps (2 meas.) precede music.

* In addition to the instruments listed on the front cover, the alto recorder may be used to play this piece.

SUITE NO. 1 IN G MINOR

1. FANTASIA

William Lawes

Transcribed and edited
by Murray Lefkowitz.

MMO 3359

25

The oboe may be used throughout this piece, except for the high C which occurs in measure 61 of this movement.

2. ON THE PLAINSONG

3. AIR

**In adddition to the instruments listed on the front cover,
the alto recorder may be used to play this piece.**

SUITE No. 3

1. PAVANE

Johann Hermann Schein

* In this performance, the final (dancers' "bow") notes have been omitted.

2. GAGLIARDE

♩ = 116   3 half note taps precede music.

3. COURANTE

♩ = 168   5 quarter note taps precede music.

4. ALLEMANDE

5. TRIPLA

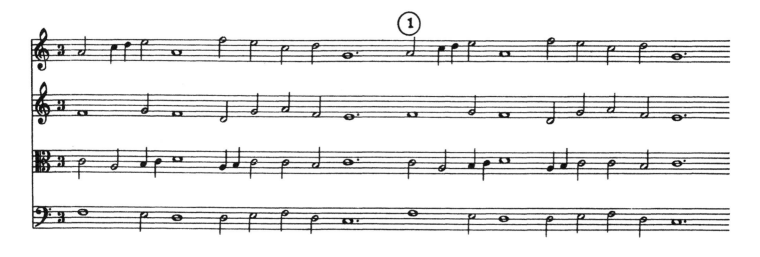

THE LEAVES BE GREEN

The Leaves Be Green - The Nuts Be Brown
They hang so high, they will not come down.

**Arranged by
Timothy Moore**

William Byrd

The original is a minor ninth lower. Note values have been halved. The dots over the crotchets should not shorten the notes too much, their only purpose being to give an accent on the following note.

* ♩. = previous ♩ (and vice-versa subsequently)

S

legato rall.

"BROWNING" FANTASY

♩ = 108   5 taps (5/6 meas.) precede music.

This setting of the popular tune "Browning" is take from Oxford Christ Church Ms.Mus.948-8. The melody which is also known as "The Leaves be greene", occurs in a substantial number of settings from the late sixteenth century, including a keyboard setting by William Inglot in the Fitzwilliam Virginal Book, a three-part ensemble version by Elway Bevin, (published in Musica Briittanica, Vol.IX), and a magnificent five-part ensemble setting by William Byrd, as well as several lute settings. In this edition the note values have been halved. Editorial accidentals appear above the stave, applying to one note only; for the sake of convenience the original accidentals are to be taken as applying to the whole bar. A fairly steady tempo is suggested, about dotted minim = 45 - 50, otherwise the quaver figures at the end, which sometimes involve quite rapid changes of harmony. will sound rushed.

MMO 3359

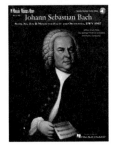    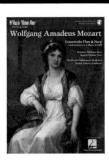  

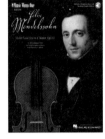

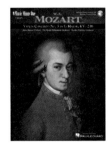

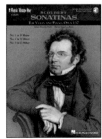